Twenty to Ma

Knitted
Headbands

Monica Russel

First published in 2015

Search Press Limited
Wellwood, North Farm Road,
Tunbridge Wells, Kent TN2 3DR

Text copyright © Monica Russel 2015

Photographs by Fiona Murray

Photographs and design copyright
© Search Press Ltd 2015

Print ISBN: 978-1-78221-159-4
ebook ISBN: 978-1-78126-244-3

The Publishers and author can accept no
responsibility for any consequences arising from
the information, advice or instructions given in
this publication.

Readers are permitted to reproduce any of the
items in this book for their personal use, or for
the purposes of selling for charity, free of charge
and without the prior permission of the Publishers.
Any use of the items for commercial purposes is
not permitted without the prior permission of
the Publishers.

Suppliers
If you have difficulty in obtaining any of the
materials and equipment mentioned in this book,
then please visit the Search Press website for
details of suppliers: www.searchpress.com

Printed in China

Dedication
To Trevor and Claerwen for their
encouragement and support.

Abbreviations

beg	beginning
dec	decrease
DPN	double-pointed needles
g st	garter stitch: knit every row
inc	increase (by working into the front and back of the same stitch)
k	knit
ktbl	knit 1 row tbl
k2tog	knit 2 stitches together
knitwise	as though to knit
m	make, usually make 1 additional stitch by knitting into the front and back of the same stitch
p	purl
p2tog	purl 2 stitches together
PM	place marker
psso	pass slipped stitch over
rem	remaining
rep	repeat
RS	right side/s
sk2po	slip 2 stitches knitwise on to right-hand needle, knit next stitch, then pass the previous slipped stitches over the knitted stitch
sl	slip, usually slip 1 stitch
ssk	slip 1 st knitwise, slip next st knitwise, insert left needle into front of both sts, knit together through back loop
st(s)	stitch(es)
st st	stocking stitch (US stockinette stitch); alternate knit and purl rows (unless directed otherwise, always start with a knit row)
tbl	through back loop
WS	wrong side/s
yrn	wrap yarn around needle to create an extra stitch. (This makes up for the stitch you lose when you knit 2 together.)
yfrn	yarn forward and over needle
yfwd	yarn forward
yo	yarn over
*	repeat the instructions following the * as many times as specified

Contents

Introduction

Headbands and headwraps are fun-to-wear accessories and will keep the chill off your head and ears whether you are cycling, walking, jogging or gardening. They are suitable for all ages and many of them are unisex. If you like a particular design, you can adapt it by making it shorter or longer, and choosing your own colour to suit an outfit, or the person you are making it for.

The patterns in this book are easy to follow and are suitable for knitters who have mastered the basics and would like to be more adventurous and try something new. They give you the chance to try out different techniques such as cables, lace, intarsia, Fair Isle and textured knitting. I have used a variety of yarns in different weights, and many of the projects can be completed in just a few hours – ideal for making a quick gift for friends and family.

I really enjoyed designing this collection. The beauty of these projects is that they are small enough to be very portable. I spent many a happy hour knitting in front of the TV, sitting in cafés, visiting friends, travelling in the car and enjoying the sunshine in the garden.

Headbands and headwraps can be worn throughout the year and add a certain panache and individuality to your wardrobe. I hope you get as much pleasure from knitting and wearing them as I have.

Knitting know-how

General notes

These knitted headbands will fit an average-sized head, apart from the Alice Flora headband, which was made for a young child. The lengths are for guidance and can be adapted to suit individual measurements. If longer ones are preferred then you will require extra yarn.

Yarn

Most yarn today comes in hanks or skeins. These are big loops of yarn that are bought by weight and thickness. Before knitting they need to be wound into a ball so that the yarn does not get knotted. Some yarns can be bought ready-prepared as balls. These come in different weights and thicknesses and you can knit directly from them.

There are a variety of yarns used in the headband projects and these can be substituted for those of your choice. It is advisable to check the length and weight of yarn that you buy against the ones used in the patterns to ensure that you have enough to finish your projects.

Lace yarn (1–3 ply) is a very fine yarn that is used for more open patterns. Generally, you get very long yardage in a 50g ball or hank. Sometimes lighter weight yarns can be doubled to create a more dense look.

DK yarn (8-ply) is a medium thickness yarn that is suitable for many projects. The main DK yarn used in these projects is made from alpaca wool, with each ball containing 120m (131yd) of yarn.

Aran yarn (10-ply) is thicker than DK yarn and will produce headbands that are thicker than those made with other weights.

Needles

Straight needles made from sustainable wood were used for all the projects in this book. I enjoy knitting with them because of their durability, and they are flexible to work with in all temperatures.

For some of the projects I used cable needles; these were also made from sustainable wood and I find that the yarns stay on them better than the metal or plastic ones.

Other materials

For all of the projects you will need a pair of good-quality, sharp scissors to cut off the ends of yarns when sewing them into your work.

As well as knitting needles, you will also need a blunt-ended needle with a large eye, such as a tapestry needle, for sewing up all your projects and weaving in any loose ends.

Mattress stitch

Mattress stitch makes a practically invisible and nicely flexible seam for joining pieces together.

1 With the right sides of the work facing, start with your yarn in the lower right corner. Take your tapestry needle across to the left edge and under the strand of yarn between the first and second stitches of the first row.

2 Take your needle back to the right edge and insert it one row up, between the first and second stitches of the row.

3 Take your needle back to the left edge and repeat stages one and two.

4 After completing a few stitches, gently pull the long end of the yarn to draw the stitches together.

This stitch will make your seam virtually invisible.

Cable cast on

This technique is used in patterns where you need to cast on in the middle of a row.

Insert your knitting needle between the first two stitches, wrap the yarn around your needle and bring it through to the front of your work. Transfer the newly created stitch onto the left-hand needle, thus increasing a stitch.

Tensions

All the tensions given for the yarns below are the manufacturer's guidelines for 10 x 10cm (4 x 4in) swatches knitted in stocking stitch (US stockinette stitch); these will be helpful if you decide to use alternative yarns to those used in the projects.

Other materials

76cm (30in) of narrow flexible jersey ribbon to sew flowers onto for the Flossie Flower headband.

Pompoms for the Flossie Flower headband (these are available in haberdashery departments and sold by the metre).

Yarns

Aran (10-ply)

West Yorkshire Spinners – Bluefaced Leicester, 100% wool.

Tension: 18 sts x 24 rows using 5mm (UK 6/US 8) knitting needles.

Yardage: 50g ball/83m/91yd; 100g ball/166m/182yd.

UK Alpaca – Baby Alpaca and Merino Blend, 80% baby alpaca, 20% superfine merino.

Tension: 19 sts x 26 rows using 4.5mm (UK 7/US 7) knitting needles.

Yardage: 1 x 50g ball/83m/91yd.

Roosters Almerino Aran – 50% alpaca, 50% merino wool.

Tension: 19 sts x 23 rows using 5mm (UK 6/US 8) knitting needles.

Yardage: 1 x 50g ball/94m/103yd.

Double Knitting (8-ply)

UK Alpaca – Superfine Alpaca, 70% alpaca, 30% Bluefaced Leicester.

Tension: 20 sts x 29 rows using 4mm (UK 8/US 6) knitting needles.

Yardage: 1 x 50g ball/120m/131yd.

UK Alpaca – Baby Alpaca, 80% baby alpaca, 20% Tussah silk.

Tension: 20 sts x 27 rows using 4mm (UK 8/US 6) knitting needles.

Yardage: 1 x 50g ball/112m/122yd.

Rooster – Almerino DK, 50% alpaca, 50% merino.

Tension: 21sts x 28 rows using 4mm (UK 8/US 6) knitting needles.

Yardage: 1 x 50g ball/113m/124yd.

Note: This is a great yarn for headbands as it has flexibility in it.

West Yorkshire Spinners – Bluefaced Leicester, 100% wool.

Tension: 22 sts x 28 rows using 4mm (UK 8/US 6) knitting needles.

Yardage: 1 x 50g ball/112m/122yd.

4-ply

UK Alpaca – Baby Alpaca and Merino Blend, 80% baby alpaca, 20% superfine merino.

Tension: 28 sts x 36 rows using 3.25mm (UK 10/US 3) knitting needles.

Yardage: 1 x 50g skein/225m/246yd.

Rooster – Lace, 80% baby alpaca, 20% silk.

Tension 20/29 sts x 33/54 rows using 2mm (UK 14/US 0) / 4mm (UK 8/US 6) knitting needles.

Yardage: 1 x 100g hank/800m/875yd.

Alice Flora

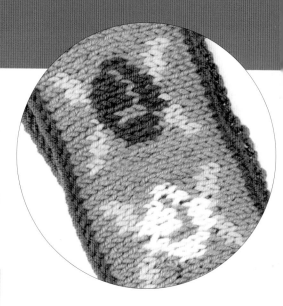

Materials:

4 x 50g balls of 100% superwash merino 4-ply yarn – 1 x pink (A), 1 x purple (B), 1 x green (C) and 1 x cream (D), each 125m/137yd

Needles:

1 pair 3mm (UK 11/US 2) single-pointed knitting needles

1 pair of 3.5mm (UK 9/US 4) single-pointed knitting needles

Knitting note

I have knitted the flowers using two colours and alternating them. You can use just one colour if you prefer.

Instructions:

Using size 3mm (UK 11/US 2) knitting needles and colour A, cast on 107 sts.

Row 1: Knit, cut off yarn A.

Change to 3.5mm (UK 9/US 4) needles.

Rows 2 and 3: st st using yarn B.

Row 4: Now set pattern as follows for row 1 of chart with spacing in between the flowers:

k1B *k1C, k7B, k1C, k3B** rep from * to ** to last 10 sts, k1C, k7B, k1C, k1B.

Now work the next 12 rows from the chart starting with a purl row, noting the knit rows (odd numbers) are worked from right to left and the purl rows are worked from left to right. Cut off yarns A and C.

Rows 17 and 18: st st using yarn B, starting with a purl row.

Cut off yarn B and rejoin yarn A. Change to 3mm (UK 11/US 2) needles.

Row 18: Knit using yarn A.

Row 19: Cast off stitches knitwise.

Making up

Weave in all loose ends. With RS facing, join side seams together using mattress stitch.

	9	8	7	6	5	4	3	2	1	
13										13
12										12
11										11
10										10
9										9
8										8
7										7
6										6
5										5
4										4
3										3
2										2
1										1

Colour A or D   Colour C

This headband has been made for a 5–8-year-old child but can easily be adapted to fit an adult.

Simple Style

Materials:

1 x 50g ball of DK superfine alpaca (8-ply) yarn in black, 120m/131yd

Needles:

1 pair of 4mm (UK 8/US 6) single-pointed knitting needles

Instructions:

Using 4mm (UK 8/US 6) knitting needles, cast on 16 sts.

Rows 1 and 2: *k2, p2, rep from * to end.

Rows 3 and 4: *p2, k2, rep from * to end.

Repeat rows 1–4 until work measures approximately 50cm (19¾in); this allows sufficient 'give' for the headband to fit snugly.

Cast off all sts.

Making up

Weave in all loose ends. With RS facing, join side seams together using mattress stitch.

This is a very simple pattern for a unisex headband made in soft alpaca that will really keep the chill away. Black is popular with men, goes with anything and always looks stylish.

Cable with Borders

Materials:

1 x 50g ball of aran yarn in red (A), 83m/91yd

1 x 100g ball of aran yarn in bullfinch (B), 166m/182yd

Needles:

1 pair of 4mm (UK 8/US 6) single-pointed knitting needles

1 pair of 5mm (UK 6/US 8) single-pointed knitting needles

1 cable needle

Instructions:

Using 4mm (UK 8/US 6) knitting needles and yarn A, cast on 104 sts, then ktbl in every st.

Rows 1 and 2: *k1, p1, rep from * to end of row.

Cut off yarn A and join yarn B.

Row 3: p16, *inc1, p12, rep from * to last 16 sts, inc1, purl to end (111 sts).

Change to 5mm (UK 6/US 8) needles and insert honeycomb pattern as follows:

Honeycomb cable

This is worked over a multiple of 11 sts.

Rows 1 and 5: p2, *k8, p3, rep from * to last 10 sts, k8, p2.

Row 2 and all even-numbered rows: k2, *p8, k3, rep from * to last 10 sts, p8, k2.

Row 3: p2, *work left crossover on 4 sts as follows: slip 2 sts to cable needle and hold in front of work, k2, k2 from cable needle; work right crossover on 4 sts as follows: slip 2 to cable needle and hold in back of work, k2, k2 from cable needle, p3, rep from * to last 10 sts, left crossover, right crossover, p2.

Row 7: p2, *right crossover, left crossover, p3, rep from * to last 10 sts, right crossover, left crossover, p2.

Row 8: k2, *p8, k3, rep from * to last 10 sts, p8, k2.

Repeat the above 8-row pattern once and then the first 4 rows once. Cut off yarn B, join yarn A.

Change to 4mm (UK 8/US 6) needles.

Next row: k15, k2tog, *k11, k2tog, rep from * to last 16 sts, k to end (104 sts).

Next 2 rows: *k1, p1, rep from * to end of row.

Cast off all sts.

Making up

With RS facing, using mattress stitch, sew up each rib using yarn A. Use yarn B to sew up the central panel. Weave in all loose ends.

This is a great headband for all the family. It will keep the chill away and look great. It can be worn to walk, ski or cycle and its width makes it a great alternative to a hat, as it keeps your ears warm.

Caramel Twist

Materials:

1 x 50g ball of DK alpaca/superfine merino in butterscotch, 112m/122yd

Needles:

1 pair 4mm (UK 8/US 6) single-pointed needles

1 cable needle

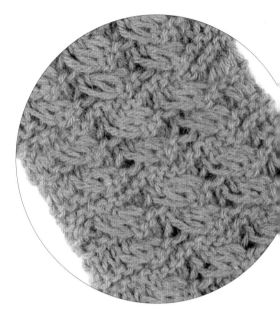

Instructions:

The lace/cable pattern is knitted in multiples of 6 + 6.

Using 4mm (UK 8/US 6) knitting needles, cast on 14 sts and ktbl in every st.

Border

Rows 1– 5: k2, inc1, knit to last 2 sts, inc1, k1 (24 sts).

Row 6: Knit.

Now insert 10-row pattern:

Rows 1 and 5 (RS): *k1, yfwd, rep from * to last st, k1 (47 sts).

Rows 2 and 6: (p1, drop yfwd from previous row) three times, *slip next 6 sts, dropping each yfwd, place these 6 sts back onto the left needle, slip the first 3 of these 6 sts onto a cable needle and leave at the front of your work, p3, then p3 from cable needle, rep from * to last 5 sts, (p1, drop yfwd) twice, p1 (24 sts).

Rows 3 and 4: Knit.

Rows 7–10: Knit.

Repeat the 10-row pattern until the headband fits around your head with a slight stretch.

Now decrease for final edge on the next 5 rows as follows:

k1, k2tog, knit to last 3 sts, k2tog, k1 (14 sts).

Knit 1 row.

Cast off all sts.

Making up

With RS facing, join side seams together using mattress stitch. Weave in all loose ends.

This pattern combines lace and cable work to produce a simple headband that can be knitted in a colour of your choice. The headband can be worn with the narrower section at the front or the back.

Diamond Fair Isle

Materials:

3 x 50g balls of DK (8-ply) alpaca/merino yarn –
1 x custard (A), 1 x smokey blue (B), 1 x burnt
orange (C), each 113m/124yd

Needles:

1 pair of 4mm (UK8/US6) single-pointed
knitting needles

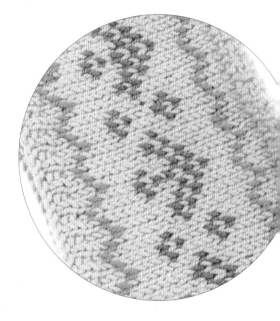

Instructions:

Using 4mm (UK 8/US 6) knitting needles and
yarn A, cast on 112 sts.

Rows 1 and 2: *k1, p1, rep from * to end.

Rows 3 and 4: st st.

Row 5: *k3A, k1B, rep from * to end.

Row 6: *p1A, p1B, rep from * to end.

Row 7: k1A, *k1B, k3A, rep from * to last 3 sts,
k1B, k2A.

Rows 8–10: Work in st st in yarn A, starting with
a purl row.

Row 11: k2A, *k1C, k5A, rep from * to last
2 sts, k1C, k1A.

Row 12: *p1C, p1A, p1C, p3A, rep from * to last
4 sts, p1C, p1A, p1C, p1A.

Row 13: k2A, k1C, *k3A, k1C, k1A, k1C, k1A,
k1C, k3A, k1C, rep from * to last st, k1A.

Row 14: p4A, *p1C, p1A, p1C, p1A, p1C, p1A,
p1C, p5A, rep from * to end.

Row 15: k4A, *k1C, k1A, k1C, k1A, k1C, k1A,
k1C, k1A, k1C, k3A, rep from * to end.

Row 16: p4A, *p1C, p5A, rep from * to end.

Rows 17 and 19: As row 11.

Row 18: As row 12.

Rows 20–22: st st.

Rows 23–25: As rows 5–7.

Rows 26–27: st st, starting with a purl row.

Rows 28–29: *k1, p1, rep from * to end.

Cast off all sts.

Making up

With RS facing, join side seams together using
mattress stitch. Weave in all loose ends.

*The simplicity of the stitch and the
spring-like colours used here really
accentuate the Fair Isle pattern.*

Dusty

Materials:

1 x 50g ball of aran baby alpaca/merino yarn in dusky pink, 94m/103yd

1 button (optional)

Needles:

1 pair of 5mm (UK 6/US 8) single-pointed knitting needles

1 pair of 4mm (UK 8/US 6) single-pointed knitting needles

Instructions:

Using size 5mm (UK 6/ US 8) knitting needles, cast on 17 sts.

Little flakes stitch

This is worked on an uneven number of stitches.

Row 1: Purl.

Row 2: Knit.

Row 3: *make 3 sts from 1 st (knit, purl, knit all into the same st), p1, rep from * to last st, work 3 sts into the last st.

Row 4: p3, *k1, p3, rep from * to end.

Row 5: k3, *p1, k3, rep from * to end.

Row 6: As row 4.

Row 7: k3tog, *p1, k3tog, rep from * to end.

Row 8: p1, *k1, p1, rep from * to end.

Row 9: p1, *knit, purl, knit all into the same st, p1, rep from * to end.

Row 10: k1, *p3, k1, rep from * to end.

Row 11: p1, *k3, p1, rep from * to end.

Row 12: As row 10.

Row 13: p1, *k3tog, p1, rep from * to end.

Row 14: k1, *p1, k1, rep from * to end.

Repeat rows 3–14 until work is long enough to fit around your head when slightly stretched.

Making up

With RS together, join the end seams using mattress stitch.

6-petal flower (optional)

Using 4mm (UK 8/US 6) needles, cast on 4 sts.

**Row 1 and every wrong side row: Purl.

Row 2 (RS): *k1, inc1, rep from * to last st, k1 (7 sts).

Row 4: *k1, inc1, rep from * to last st, k1 (13 sts).

Row 6: Knit.

Row 8: k5, sk2po, k5 (11 sts).

Row 10: k4, sk2po, k4 (9 sts).

Row 12: k3, sk2po, k3 (7 sts).

Row 13: Purl.

Cut yarn leaving a reasonable length and leave the 7 sts on the needle.

On the second needle, cast on 4 sts and rep from ** five more times (six petals in total), leaving RS facing for the next row (42 sts in total on needle).

Continue as follows:

Row 14 (RS): k6, k2tog, *k5, k2tog, rep from * 3 more times, k6 (37 sts).

Row 15: *p2tog, rep from * to last st, p1 (19 sts).

Row 16: Knit.

Row 17: *p2tog, rep from * to last st, p1 (10 sts).

Row 18: *k2tog, rep from * to end (5 sts).

Row 19: Pass second, third, fourth and fifth sts over the first stitch.

Cut yarn, and pass through remaining st.

Making up

Pull up ends at the base of each petal and then using each end in turn, sew adjacent petals together to approximately 1.5cm (½in) from the base. Sew in all ends of yarn by weaving them into the back of the work.

Sew the button onto the centre of the flower and then sew the flower onto the headband. Attach the tips of the top and bottom petals to the headband to prevent the flower flopping over.

This textured headband is made from a super soft yarn in a subtle colour. I have added a flower for fun and to give it a vintage look.

Dynamic Wave

Materials:
2 x 50g balls of DK alpaca/merino yarn – 1 x grey (A), 1 x dusky pink (B), each 113m/124yd

Needles:
1 pair of 4mm (UK 8/US 6) single-pointed knitting needles

Knitting note
When working from the chart, please note that the knit rows are the odd-numbered rows and the purl rows are the even-numbered rows. Remember to twist yarn every 3–4 sts to avoid large loops at the back of your work.

Instructions:
Using size 4mm (UK 8/US 6) knitting needles and yarn A, cast on 28 sts and ktbl to form a neat edge.

Join yarn B and continue by working the 10-row pattern from the chart below until work measures approximately 46cm (18in). This allows for some 'give' when placed around an adult's head.

Fasten off yarn B.

Knit 1 row in yarn A.

Cast off all sts.

Making up
With RS facing, join side seams together using mattress stitch. Weave in all loose ends.

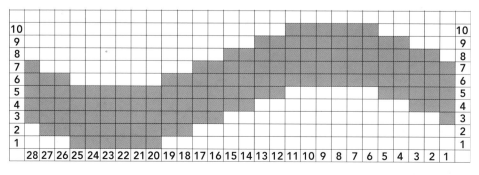

This is a great headband for all ages. Simply choose your favourite colours and away you go.

Lacy Fern

Materials:

1 x 100g hank of lace weight alpaca/silk in fern green, 800m/875yd

Needles:

1 pair 3mm (UK 11/US 2) single-pointed knitting needles

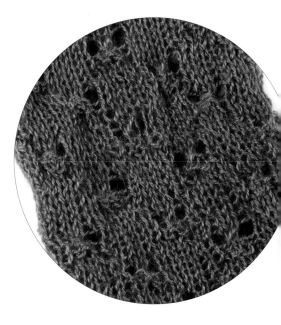

Instructions:

The lace pattern is knitted in multiples of 8 + 5.

Using 3mm (UK 11/US 2) knitting needles, cast on 37 sts.

Row 1 (RS): Knit.

Row 2: Purl.

Row 3: k1, p3, *k5, p3, rep from * to last st, k1.

Row 4: p1, k3, *p5, k3, rep from * to last st, p1.

Row 5: k1, yfrn, k3tog, yfrn, *k5, yfrn, k3tog, yfrn, rep from * to last st, k1.

Rows 6–8: Stocking stitch starting with a purl row.

Row 9: k5, *p3, k5, rep from * to end.

Row 10: p5, *k3, p5, rep from * to end.

Row 11: k5, *yfrn, k3tog, yfrn, k5, rep from * to end.

Row 12: Purl.

Repeat these 12 rows until the headband fits snugly around your head with a slight stretch, ending with either a row 6 or a row 12.

Cast off all sts.

Making up

With RS of work together, join seams together using mattress stitch. Weave in all loose ends.

Twist it, fold it or wear it flat – this headwrap is very versatile. The lacy stitch gives the band movement, so you can create your own look.

Flossie Flower

Materials:

3 x 50g balls of DK (8-ply) baby alpaca/merino
yarn – 1 x pink, 1 x cream, 1 x orange, each
113m/124yd

5 x small, ready-made pompoms for the
flower centres

I length of stretchy jersey as the base for the
headband, approx. 76cm (30in) long for a
child/young adult's head, plus extra for tying.
Alternatively, use a ready-made headband.

Needles:

1 pair of 4mm (UK 8/US 6) single-pointed
knitting needles

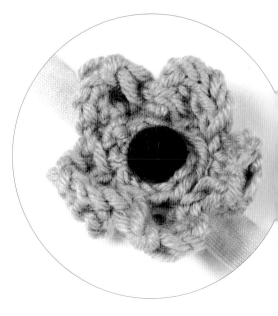

Instructions:

Flowers

Make five. Using colour of your choice and 4mm
(UK 8/US 6) knitting needles, cast on 4 sts.

Row 1: k4.

Row 2: In the first st (k1, p1, k1tbl, p1, k1tbl), turn,
k5, turn, p5, turn, k5, turn, p2tog twice, p1. Place
the yarn to the back of your work, slip the second
and third sts over the first stitch.

Row 3: Purl 3 remaining sts on left-hand needle.

Repeat rows 1–3 three times and then rows 1 and
2 once more. Cast off remaining sts purlwise.

Making up

Weave in all loose ends. Sew the cast-on edge
and cast-off edge of each flower together. Sew
one pompom in the centre of each flower.

Sew one flower in the centre of the length of
jersey and space the other four 6cm (2¼in) apart
across the front of the band. The two ends can be
knotted together once the band is on your head.

*This headband is reminiscent of spring
flowers and bursts of colour after the
winter months, and the flowers are quick
and easy to make. The finished headband
will fit a teenager or young adult, and can
be easily adapted to fit any size.*

Forties' Style

Materials:

2 x 50g balls of DK superfine alpaca (8-ply) yarn
in parchment, each 120m/131yd

Needles:

1 pair of 4mm (UK 8/US 6) single-pointed
knitting needles

Instructions:

Using 4mm (UK 8/US 6) knitting needles, cast
on 28 sts.

Row 1: Knit.

Row 2: k11tbl, turn.

Rows 3 and 5: Knit.

Row 4: k22tbl, turn.

Row 6: ktbl in every st.

Row 7: k1, inc1 in next st, knit to last 3 sts,
k2tog, k1.

Repeat rows 6 and 7 until piece measures 25cm
(9¾in) at the longest point, ending with row 6.

Now continue as follows:

Row 1: k1, (k2tog) 13 times, k1 (15 sts).

Row 2: ktbl in every st.

Row 3: k1, inc1 in next st, knit to last 3 sts,
k2tog, k1.

Repeat rows 2 and 3 until work measures 62cm
(24½in) at the longest edge, ending with row 2
of pattern.

Now continue as follows:

Row 1: k1, inc1 in each of the next 13 sts, k1 (28
sts).

Row 2: ktbl in every st.

Row 3: k1, inc1 in next st, knit to last 3 sts,
k2tog, k1.

Repeat rows 2 and 3 until work measures 82cm
(32¼in) at the longest edge, ending with row 2
of pattern.

Next row: k22, turn.

Next row: ktbl in every st.

Next row: k11, turn.

Next row: ktbl in every st.

Cast off all sts.

Making up

After completing the knitting, block your work.
Lay the headband flat with the underside facing
you. Fold both side edges into the middle,
starting from where the stitches are increased
on one end and decreased on the other end,
leaving the centre panel as a single piece of
knitting. Press the sides lightly with an iron, so
that the seam is down the middle of the band.
Sew the seams together using mattress stitch.
Weave in all loose ends. Finally, tie a knot (left
end over right end, twist one end under and
then right over left).

*This headband is a replica of one that
factory workers wore in the 1940s. It is
knitted in a luxurious DK alpaca yarn.*

Gentleman's Relish

Materials:

1 x 100g ball of DK (8-ply) yarn in self-patterning
   blue, grey, yellow and cream, 224m/245yd

Needles:

1 pair of 4mm (UK 8/US 6) single-pointed
   knitting needles

Instructions:

Using 4mm (UK 8/US 6) knitting needles, cast
on 18 sts.

Row 1 and odd-numbered rows: Knit.

Row 2 and even-numbered rows: k3, purl to last
3 sts, k3.

Repeat these two rows until work is long enough
to fit around your head when stretched slightly.

Cast off all sts.

Making up

With RS of work together, join seams together
using mattress stitch. Weave in all loose ends.

*This unisex headband is very simple to
make but looks more complex because
of the self-patterning yarn, which
creates an attractive design.*

Gooseberry

Materials:

1 x 50g ball of DK (8-ply) merino/alpaca yarn in gooseberry, 113m/124yd

2 x buttons

Needles:

1 pair of 4mm (UK 8/US 6) single-pointed knitting needles

Instructions:

Using size 4mm (UK 8/US 6) needles, cast on 9 sts and ktbl in every st.

Row 1 (buttonhole row): k4, cast off 2 sts, knit to end.

Row 2: k3, cast on 2 sts using cable cast on method, k4.

Row 3: inc1, knit to last st, inc1 (11 sts).

Row 4: p1, *yrn, p2tog, rep from * to end.

Repeat rows 3 and 4 until there are 17 sts.

Lace pattern

Row 1 (RS): sl1, yfrn, k3, sl1, k1, psso, p5, k2tog, k3, yfrn, k1.

Row 2: sl1, p5, k5, p6.

Row 3: sl1, k1, yfrn, k3, sl1, k1, psso, p3, k2tog, k3, yfrn, k2.

Row 4: sl1, p6, k3, p7.

Row 5: sl1, k2, yfrn, k3, sl1, k1, psso, p1, k2tog, k3, yfrn, k3.

Row 6: sl1, p7, k1, p8.

Row 7: sl1, k3, yfrn, k3, sl1, k2tog, psso, k3, yfrn, k4.

Row 8: sl1, purl to last st.

Repeat the last 8 rows until work measures 46cm (18in) or desired length, and is long enough to go around your head with a slight stretch (ending on a row 8).

Row 1: k1, k2tog, knit to last 3 sts, k2tog, k1 (15 sts).

Row 2: p1, *yfrn, p2tog, rep from * to end.

Repeat the last 2 rows until there are 9 sts.

Next row: Knit.

Cast off all sts.

Making up

Sew a button on the cast-off end to correspond with the buttonhole on the cast-on end. Sew another button in the centre of the front (optional). Weave in all loose ends.

This neat, decorative headband is great for all ages. Simply knit it to the length required (it should fit snugly around the head with a bit of stretch) and add a pretty button as a detail.

Head in the Clouds

Materials:

2 x 50g balls of DK baby alpaca/Tussah silk
yarn – 1 x china blue (A), 1 x lunar grey (B),
each 112m/12yd

Needles:

1 pair of 4mm (UK 8/US 6) single-pointed
knitting needles

Instructions:

Using size 4mm (UK 8/US 6) needles and yarn A, cast
on 100 sts, then ktbl to form a neat edge.

Rows 1 and 2: *k1, p1, rep from * to end.

Row 3: k2, k2tog, knit to last 4 sts, k2tog, k2 (98 sts).

Row 4: Knit.

Row 5: Change to yarn B, knit.

Row 6: Using yarn B, k10, *p10, turn, k10, turn, p9, turn,
k8, turn, p9, k24, rep from * once more, p10, turn, k10,
turn, p9, turn, k8, turn, p9, k10.

Rows 7–10: Using yarn A, knit.

Row 11: Using yarn B, knit.

Row 12: Using yarn B, k27, p10, turn, k10, turn, p9,
turn, k8, turn, p9, k24, p10, turn, k10, turn, p9, turn, k8,
turn, p9, k27.

Rows 13–16: Knit using yarn A.

Now repeat rows 5–12 once more.

Knit 2 rows using yarn A.

Next 2 rows: Using yarn A, *k1, p1, rep from * to end.

Cast off all sts.

Making up

With RS facing, join seams together using mattress
stitch. Weave in all loose ends.

*This headband has a textured pattern
within a garter stitch surround. I have used
muted colours, but the look could be
completely changed by using bright ones.*

Springtime

Materials:

1 x 50g ball of alpaca/merino DK in orange,
113m/124yd

Needles:

1 pair of 4mm (UK 8/US 6) single-pointed
knitting needles

1 cable needle

Instructions:

Using 4mm (UK 8/US 6) needles cast on 17 sts.

Work in st st until work measures 14.5cm (5¾in).

Cable pattern

Rows 1, 3 and 7: p2, k6, p1, k6, p2.

Rows 2 and all even rows: k2, p6, k1, p6, k2.

Row 5: p2, slip 3 sts onto cable needle and hold at back
of work, k3, k3 from cable needle, p1, slip 3 sts to cable
needle and hold at front of work, k3, k3 from cable
needle, p2.

Repeat the 8-row cable pattern until work measures
37cm (14½in), ending on row 8 of pattern. Place a
marker in the middle of the row. Continue working in st
st for another 15cm (6in) from marker.

Cast off all sts.

Making up

With RS facing, join side seams together using mattress
stitch. Weave in all loose ends.

*A yarn that has some stretch is great for
this project, so that it fits snugly around
your head. The combination of stocking
stitch and a cable makes the front
narrower than the sides and back.*

Versatile Mesh

Materials:

1 x 50g hank of 4-ply silk/merino yarn in variegated cream and purple, 225m/246yd

Needles:

1 pair 3.25mm (UK 10/US 3) single-pointed knitting needles

Instructions:

Using size 3.25mm (UK 10/US 3) needles, cast on 57 sts.

Row 1: k1, *yfrn, k2tog, rep from * to end.

Row 2: Purl.

Row 3: * sl1, k1, psso, yfrn, rep from * to last st, k1.

Row 4: Purl.

Repeat these 4 rows until work fits snugly when stretched around your head.

Cast off all sts.

Making up

With RS together, join seams together using mattress stitch. Weave in all loose ends.

This is a really versatile headband that can be worn in numerous ways – twist it, wrap it and play around to create the look you like. It is knitted with a silky, 4-ply variegated yarn in a lacy stitch to make it very flexible.

Red Robin

Materials:

1 x 50g ball of Bluefaced Leicester aran wool in red, 83m/91yd

Needles:

1 pair of 5mm (UK 6/US 8) single-pointed knitting needles

1 cable needle

Instructions:

Using 5mm (UK 6/US 8) needles, cast on 87 sts, then ktbl to form a neat edge.

Row 1: k1, p2tog, *k1, p1, rep from * to last 3 sts, p2tog, k1 (85 sts).

Row 2: * k1, p1, rep from * to end.

Insert pattern as follows (the pattern is repeated five times across each row as a 17-st pattern repeat):

Row 1 (RS): * p6, k2tog, yfrn, p1, yo, sl1, k1, psso, p6, rep from * to end.

Row 2: *k6, p1, k3, p1, k6, rep from * to end.

Row 3: *p5, k2tog, yfrn, p3, yo, sl1, k1, psso, p5, rep from * to end.

Row 4: *(k5, p1) twice, k5, rep from * to end.

Row 5: *p4, k2tog, yfrn, (p1, k1) twice, p1, yo, sl1, k1, psso, p4, rep from * to end.

Row 6: *k4, p1, k2, p1, k1, p1, k2, p1, k4, rep from * to end.

Row 7: *p3, k2tog, yfrn, p2, k1, p1, k1, p2, yo, sl1, k1, psso, p3, rep from * to end.

Row 8: *(k3, p1) twice, k1, (p1, k3) twice, rep from * to end.

Row 9: *p2, k2tog, yfrn, p2, k2tog, yfrn, p1, yo, sl1, k1, psso, p2, yo, sl1, k1, psso, p2, rep from * to end.

Row 10: *k2, (p1, k3) three times, p1, k2, rep from * to end.

Row 11 (Bobble row): *p2, (k1, p1, k1, p1) into next st, turn, p4, turn, k4, turn, p4, turn, sl1, k1, psso, k2tog, turn, p2tog, turn, slip bobble onto right-hand needle (bobble completed), p2, k2tog, yfrn, p3, yo, sl1, k1, psso, p2, make second bobble and slip it onto right-hand needle, p2, rep from * to end.

Row 12: As row 4.

Row 13: k1, p2tog, *k1, p1, rep from * to last 3 sts, k2tog, p1 (83 sts).

Row 14: *k1, p1, rep from * to end.

Cast off all sts.

Making up

With RS facing, join seams together using mattress stitch. Weave in all loose ends.

This headband combines lace with bobbles. It is knitted in bright red to give it a festive feel.

Snowflake

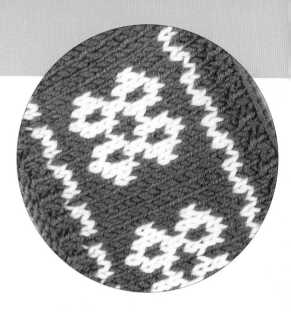

Materials:

2 x 50g balls of DK (8-ply) merino/alpaca yarn – 1 x slate grey (A), 1 x ivory (B), each 113m/124yd

Needles:

1 pair of 4mm (UK 8/US 6) single-pointed knitting needles

1 x stitch marker

Instructions:

Using size 4mm (UK 8/US 6) needles and colour A, cast on 108 sts, then ktbl to form a neat edge.

Rows 1 and 2: *k1, p1, rep from * to end.

Row 3: *k3B, k1A, rep from * to end.

Row 4: p2B, *p1A, p3B, rep from * to last 2 sts, p1A, p1B.

Row 5: Knit in A.

Row 6: Purl in A.

Row 7: Work chart row 1 eight times across row in knit, k4A.

Continue working from the chart; odd-numbered rows are knitted and worked from right to left, and even-numbered rows are purled working from left to right.

Next row: Purl in A.

Next row: Knit in A.

Next row: *p1A, p3B, rep from * to end.

Next row: k1B, *k1A, k3B, rep from * to last 3 sts, k1A, k2B.

Cut off yarn B.

Next row: Purl.

Next row: Knit.

Work next 2 rows as rows 1 and 2 of pattern.

Cast off.

Making up

With RS facing, join seams together using mattress stitch. Weave in all loose ends.

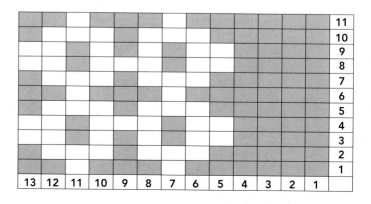

This headband will complement any winter outfit in these soft, neutral colours.

Lacy Dream

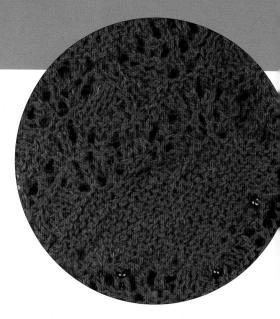

Materials:

1 x 50g hank of 4-ply baby alpaca/superfine merino in cobalt blue, 225m/246yd

Small beads for the borders

Needles:

1 pair of 3.25mm (UK 10/US 3) single-pointed knitting needles

Knitting note

Cut off six long lengths of yarn prior to casting on, to work the beads in. While knitting your pattern, use a long end of yarn at either side of the headband and knit it as you go along – this makes it easy to thread in your beads using a narrow-eyed needle. I found it helpful to knit the first and last stitch of alternate rows with both the yarn from the main pattern and the end yarn, to avoid loops up the side of the work.

Instructions:

Using 3.25mm (UK 10/US 3) needles, cast on 3 sts. Sew in one bead at the point of your work.

Row 1: Knit.

Row 2: k1, inc1, k1, inc1, k1 (5 sts).

Row 3: Knit.

Row 4: k2, inc1, knit to last st, inc1, k1 (7 sts).

Repeat the last 2 rows until there are 29 sts, inserting a bead at either side of the work on row 12.

Next row: Knit.

Next row: k2, inc1, knit to end (30 sts).

Continue in the following lace pattern, inserting one bead at each end on every first row of pattern sequence.

Rows 1–4: Knit.

Row 5: k2, *sl1, k1, psso, k4, yfrn, k1, yfrn, k4, k2tog, rep from * to last 2 sts, k2.

Rows 6, 8, 10 and 12: Purl.

Row 7: k2, *sl1, k1, psso, (k3, yfrn) twice, k3, k2tog, rep from * to last 2 sts, k2.

Row 9: k2, *sl1, k1, psso, k2, yfrn, k2tog, yfrn, k1, yfrn, sl1, k1, psso, yfrn, k2, k2tog, rep from * to last 2 sts, k2.

Row 11: k2, *sl1, k1, psso, k1, yfrn, k2tog, yfrn, k3, yfrn, sl1, k1, psso, yfrn, k1, k2tog, rep from * to last 2 sts, k2.

Row 13: k2, *sl1, k1, psso, (yfrn, k2tog) twice, yfrn, k1, (yfrn, sl1, k1, psso) twice, yfrn, k2tog, rep from * to last 2 sts, k2.

Row 14: Purl.

Continue the 14-row pattern repeat until the headband fits snugly around your head, ending with row 4 of the pattern.

Cast off all sts.

Making up

Block work carefully. With RS facing, place the shaped end (cast-on end) over the cast-off edge and sew in place. Turn the work over and sew the seam at the back to secure it. Weave in all loose ends.

The softness of the yarn and the lacy stitch used here combine to make this a luxurious headband, with a touch of glamour provided by the beads along the borders.

Two-tone Cable

Materials:

- 1 x 50g ball of DK Bluefaced Leicester in black/brown tweed look (A), 102m/112yd
- 1 x 50g ball of DK superfine alpaca yarn in black (B), 120m/131yd

Needles:

- 1 pair of 4mm (UK 8/US 6) single-pointed knitting needles
- 1 x cable needle

Instructions:

Using 4mm (UK 8/US 6) needles and yarn A, cast on 29 sts, then ktbl to form a neat edge.

Note: the first 10 and last 10 sts are worked in yarn A and the middle 9 sts in yarn B.

Cable pattern

Remember to twist yarns every time you change colours to avoid gaps in your knitting.

Rows 1 and 5: k10A, k9B, k10A.

Rows 2, 4, 6 and 8: k1A, p9A, p9B, p9A, k1A.

Row 3: k1A, *slip next 3 sts onto a cable needle and hold at back of work, k3A, k3A from cable needle**, k3A, rep from * to ** in yarn B, k3B, rep from * to ** in yarn A, k4A.

Row 7: k4A, *slip 3 sts onto a cable needle and hold at front of work, k3A, k3A from cable needle**, k3B, rep from * to ** in yarn B, k3A, rep from * to ** in yarn A, k1A.

Continue the 8-row cable pattern until the headband fits snugly around your head with a slight stretch, ending on row 8 of pattern.

Knit 1 row in yarn A.

Cast off all sts.

Making up

With RS facing, join seams together using mattress stitch. Weave in all loose ends.

I have used a two-tone cable for this pattern to give it a certain panache. If preferred, it could be done in a single colour. This headband is particularly versatile and would suit all family members.

Ziggy

Materials:

1 x 50g ball of aran baby alpaca/superfine merino in lunar grey, 83m/91yd

1 large button

Needles:

1 pair of 4.5mm (UK 7/US 7) single-pointed knitting needles

Instructions:

Using size 4.5mm (UK 7/US 7) needles, cast on 8 sts, then ktbl to form a neat edge.

Rows 1–4: Knit.

Rows 5, 9, 13, 17: k2, inc1, knit to last 2 sts, k1, inc1, k1.

Rows 6–8: Knit.

Rows 10–12: Knit.

Rows 14–16: Knit.

Row 18: Knit (16 sts).

Right slant

Row 1: K1, *yo, k2tog, rep from * to last st, k1.

Row 2: Purl.

Repeat these 2 rows another four times.

Left slant

Row 1: k1, *ssk, yo, rep from * to last st, k1.

Row 2: Purl.

Repeat rows 1 and 2 another four times.

You will now continue to work the right-slant pattern five times then the left-slant pattern five times until work fits snugly around your head (with a slight stretch), ending with a row 10 of the left-slant pattern.

Now start decreasing as follows:

Rows 1–2: Knit.

Rows 3, 7, 11: k1, k2tog, knit to last 3 stitches, k2tog, k1.

Rows 4–6, 8–10, and 12: Knit.

Row 13 (buttonhole row): k4, cast off 3 sts, knit to end.

Row 14: Knit, casting on 3 sts over the cast-off sts.

Rows 15 and 16: Knit.

Row 17: k1, k2tog, knit to last 3 sts, k2tog, k1.

Row 18: Knit.

Cast off all sts.

Making up

Weave in all loose ends. Sew on button.

This is a great project to make in an evening – simply choose your favourite colour in a soft yarn. The headband can be worn with the button at the side or the back.

Acknowledgements

My special thanks to John and Pete at Rooster
yarns for their generosity in supplying me with a
wide range of colourful yarns to play around with
for many of the projects. My thanks also go to
Chas and Rachel at UK Alpaca for their ongoing
support of my design work and their contribution
of yarns. Finally, thanks to the team at West
Yorkshire Spinners for supplying some of the yarn
for my projects. And, of course, a huge thank you
to my editor May Corfield and the team at
Search Press, who have enabled me
to produce my fourth book for them.
For yarns and other patterns,
visit the author's website:
www.the knitknacks.co.uk

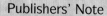

Publishers' Note

If you would like more information on knitting techniques try:
Knitting for the Absolute Beginner by Alison Dupernex,
Search Press, 2012;
Twenty to Make: Easy Knitted Scarves by Monica Russel,
Search Press, 2013